Artisans Of The Crucifixion

A Dramatic Program For Lent

Jeffrey R. Ingold

CSS Publishing Company, Inc., Lima, Ohio

Scripture quotations are from the *New Revised Standard Version of the Bible*, copyright 1989 by the Division of Christian Education of the National Council of the Churches of Christ in the USA. Used by permission.

ISBN: 0-7880-1313-0

This book is dedicated to Jennifer, my spouse. She supports me in my creative efforts and for this I love her and thank God for her.

Table Of Contents

Introduction

The following is a program to be presented during the season of Lent. The program includes five consecutive dramatic presentations portraying the fictitious people who were the artisans of certain items used at Christ's Passion. Five poems support the theme of each presentation. They may be incorporated into a worship service preceding each presentation. Author's suggestions as to the way the program may be presented, complete with recommendations about keepsake items that may be handed out to the congregation at each presentation, are also included.

During the first dramatic presentation the audience will meet the person who was responsible for crafting the whip with which our Lord Jesus was flogged. Secondly, they will meet the basket weaver who helped the soldiers twist the crown of thorns which was thrust down upon Jesus' head. The audience will hear next from the blacksmith who forged the nails by which Jesus Christ was fastened to the cross. Then they will listen as the carpenter of that instrument of torture and death on which Jesus hung — the cross — tells his story. Finally, the audience will listen and watch as the stone mason who chiseled out the tomb where Jesus' body was laid shares his story. In each instance, the artisans, who are laboring over their craft throughout the presentation, will share their perspective on the events surrounding Jesus' Passion. The dramatic presentations are about fictitious artisans of the day who, though they may not have actually been in a position to view each event for themselves any more than you or I, were still deeply involved in the event of Jesus' humiliation and death, the same as you and I. In essence, the stories of the artisans may help us better relate to our own stories.

The actor(s) can be as elaborate as they care to be in presenting each drama. However, I suggest it would be beneficial to the overall effect if, at the very least, a few props offering a sense of authenticity were used in each presentation. The impact each drama attempts to achieve is the suggestion that the artisans who are telling their stories are doing it from their own workshops while engaged in the activity of their artistry.

For example, in the portrayal of "The Tanner" who crafted the whip, a whip ought to be on hand to demonstrate its cracking sound. There is a place in the script which allows for such a demonstration. Also, animal hides and skins may be placed around the staging area where the drama is being presented. Additionally, you may simulate tanning an animal hide during the presentation to enhance the suggestion of authenticity.

When presenting "The Basket Maker" who twisted the crown of thorns, the actress or actor will simulate weaving a basket during the presentation. Baskets and basket-making material may be strewn around the staging areas. A crown of thorns will be necessary as it will be used in the presentation. Several branches from a crab apple tree may be used to twist the crown. Preferably, find a tree which has dropped some branches or has been felled in a storm, then utilize the dead branches. Soak the branches for 48 hours to make them pliable for weaving into a crown. Simply braid two branches to begin with, completing a 10" circle. Then weave additional branches into your braid until you are satisfied with your crown of thorns.

For the presentation of "The Blacksmith" who crafted the nails, it will be effective if forged nails could be borrowed from an area smithy along with a real anvil, a smith's hammer, and tongs with which the presenter can simulate pounding out a nail. The resulting clang of metal upon metal indicated at points throughout the script is effective. The presenter could also smudge black soot over face, arms, and costume so the sense of authenticity may be achieved.

It will be effective for the presentation of "The Carpenter" for the cross to have a few ancient-looking carpentry tools scattered around the staging area and used in the presentation, especially a planing tool. Two large cross beams will be put together during this presentation. I recommend that you acquire a 12' piece of 4" x 4" lumber. Cut it into a 7' length and a 5' length. Measure to the 5' mark on the longer piece of lumber and from that mark cut a notch the width of the lumber, halfway through the beam. Then measure to the halfway mark on the shorter beam and cut a notch the width of the lumber, halfway through this board. Make certain that you measure the width of the beam accurately to find the center, then measure back one-half the width to begin your cut on the shorter length. The two beams should now fit together where the notches have been cut (some sanding or filing may be necessary to adjust the fit), and it should take the shape of a cross. In the presentation, the actor will simulate planing the wood, then putting the beams together and binding them tightly with rope to finish making the cross.

Finally, if "The Stonemason" is actually chiseling on a large chunk of stone with finished blocks and scraps of masonry scattered around, the suggestion of authenticity will be achieved. Locate an article that looks like a column. It may be a planter, or a stand, or a garden ornament. This piece will be used for display only in the presentation. Then place a piece of stone, on which you do not mind chiseling, behind the decorative column. Using a hammer and a chisel to chip away at the stone behind the column, the presenter may create the illusion that he is actually chiseling the back of the decorative piece. The sounds and the action will add to the effect of the drama. Throughout these dramatic presentations, the actor(s) may utilize costumes that will give the suggestion of Jesus' day.

Additionally, the drama will be most effective as a more complete experience when samples from each presentation are given to each person in the congregation during a worship service preceding each presentation. These tangible keepsake items, combined with the congregational reading of the poems (included in the appendix), will help the participants to connect more fully with the thoughts and emotions which the dramas, and the season of Lent, may evoke.

You may use a swatch of leather for the presentation of "The Tanner." These can be found in any craft store as suede fringe and then handed out to the congregation. Small branches of thorns may be cut about 3" long to give to the congregation. These may be cut from what is left over after making the crown for the presentation of "The Basket Maker." Masonry nails may be purchased at a home improvement store to be distributed at the presentation of "The Blacksmith." A rough wooden cross (palm size) made out of dowel rods can be produced by someone in your congregation, then given to each person at the presentation of "The Carpenter." Finally, small pieces of sandstone should be given to the congregation for the presentation of "The Stone Mason." Any home improvement store or concrete company will have such stones.

The Testimony Of The Tanner

(The actor is stretching or brushing an animal hide as the drama begins. A few ancient-looking tools and furs are scattered around the work area.)

He sure was in a pretty big hurry. The soldier from the Roman guard, I mean. He just left here ... you may have passed him on your way in! He came here all in an uproar over some Jesse ... or Jesu ... uh, some man stirring up a lot a trouble. Something about being some king of the Jewish people. Well, that's what this guard said anyway ... and he came here all anxious, looking for one of my special whips ... like this one, except more dangerous. *(He holds up the whip and cracks it.)* I wonder what's going on over at the governor's place that someone should deserve a beating from one of my special whips. You see, the one he took ... the whip, I mean ... like I said, it's a special kind. I'd hate to be the unlucky sport they exercise that one on. I say it's special because it has sharp stones sewn into the ends of the talons that gouge the flesh. Oh, it's wicked! *(Almost to himself)* I hope it's not that Jesse or Jesu ... JESUS! Yeah, that's what the soldier said his name is ... Jesus. Says he's another one of those self-proclaimed Messiah/Savior kings, I guess. *(Shrugs)* So, what's the big deal? They come around all the time claiming to be someone they are not. He can't be hurting anyone. Besides, they only use my special whips on the most hardened of criminals like murderers and political insurrectionists. *(Pauses briefly as he appears lost in thought. He then continues to work the animal hide.)* What's the harm in people playing like they're a Messiah/Savior or king? Some people take their religion a little too far. I've never heard about him starting any war or anything. Surely this Jesus can't deserve ... *(Perplexed)* Why would they want one of my whips?

(His mood begins suddenly to grow agitated and defensive.) You know, a lot of people get upset with me because I make these whips. You might be one of them. People come down on me all the

time telling me I'm encouraging violence by producing these instruments of pain and torture. *(His voice indicates his growing agitation. Suddenly, he picks up the whip and takes two aggressive steps toward the audience ... yet his voice belies a tinge of guilt.)* Well, I'll tell you what ... like I always say, "Whips don't hurt people! People hurt people using whips!" *(He pauses for effect, holding the whip out toward the audience. He then drops the whip to his side and shrugs with a "who cares" attitude and, placing the whip in a place where the audience can still see it, he goes back to working the animal hide.)* Besides ... whether you like it or not, there's a good market for these whips with the military and the fact is, I have to make a living. So nobody can make me feel like what goes on up there at the governor's palace today, or anytime those soldiers decide to use my whips, is somehow my fault. *(Still agitated)* No way! And if they decide to whip that man Jesus until his back is gaping open ... hey, that's their business. His blood isn't on my hands. I have nothing to do with that! *(His tone changes toward one who is pleading his case, and again his voice belies his deeply felt shame.)* Look, I take too much pride in my craft to let anybody get me down about what someone else does with it. *(He takes a long pause as he feverishly works the animal hide until he calms. He becomes lost in thought again.)* Still and all, I hope it isn't that Jesus fella. From what the soldier said, it doesn't make any sense. I mean, I can't believe that he would have done anything to deserve a beating with one of my *(catches himself with a pang of guilt in his voice)* ... one of *(with emphasis) those* special whips.

He did say something strange while he was here, now that I think about it ... the soldier, I mean. Well, we kind of had a few minutes to talk. Even though he was in a real big hurry to get the whip and go, I wasn't quite finished putting the handle on it when he got here. Anyway, one of the things the guard said was that this Jesus fella ... this king of sorts ... seemed to have an extraordinary amount of people shouting for Pilate, the governor, to crucify him. The strange thing is, as far as I know, they never beat a man, especially with one of my ... *(catches himself again)* ... those special whips and then hang him. That's completely unheard of. And yet the guard said that all this Jesus fellow is accused of is being the

Messiah — like a savior or something. I guess the religious leaders want to trump him up on criminal charges of blasphemy and insubordination. That must be where the reference to him being a king comes from. *(More thoughtfully)* But still, a flogging and then a crucifixion just for claiming to be a king? What possible harm could there be in that?

Not only that, but something else the guard said before I finished the whip for him was that this Jesus fella ... seems to only have a handful of supporters who are willing to stand up for him there at the governor's place. He said that when they arrested this Jesus, most of his regular followers who were with him in some garden on the other side of town last night — Gethsemane — ran away. It sounds like they deserted him. Apparently those who didn't, the ones up in the governor's palace with him right now ... well, as the guard puts it, "they are a bunch of weeping women and a few weakling men." What kind of a guy is this anyway? Only the scruff of society seems to pay any mind to his claim that he really is a Savior or a king. A bunch of weaklings. It all sounds pretty ridiculous if you ask me. I mean, if the Roman guard were about to tear my back open with one of those whips and then nail me to a cross, you better believe I would drop the whole business about being the Messiah real fast. Wouldn't you? *(Starting to get agitated again)* I don't care how devout one is to his religion or his belief, if someone was going to kill you for it, you would have to be pretty crazy to stick to your story. Hey, don't get me wrong. I'll be the first one to tell you I believe in God, but come on ... if you say you're going to kill me for it ... watch me run. Who needs that? And those weepy women and little men who are standing by this Jesus ... well, all I can say is they must be nuts too. *(Convincingly, with a false sense of pride)* I'm just glad I don't have anything to do with that mess up there. Even if it is one of those special whips I make that they will use on him. *(Pauses, thinking about what he said and becoming defensive again)* Th ... that doesn't ... mean ... I'm involved ... Okay ... *(turns accusingly)* at least not any more than any of you. I don't see any of you standing up for him!

(Working the hide) Still, I can't help but think that something just isn't right about what's going on up there at the governor's

13

place. I mean, either that Jesus is a total fool ... or, he's for real. And why those few women and men would stay with him through all that ... I don't care how strong their belief in him is, I know I wouldn't be able to stick with him ... it looks like it would be too dangerous ... too frustrating for my tastes. *(His thought process is gaining momentum.)* Hey, if I was going to sink my belief and my life into someone who is claiming to be the savior of the people, I would want to know without any doubt that that someone is for real. What about you? Wouldn't you want to know he's for real before you choose to put your reputation on the line for him? Your life? I mean, would you put your trust in someone who was just going to stand there and take all that abuse from those soldiers and who would let all those other people go ahead and rally for his death? You'd think he'd at least apologize for the whole big misunderstanding and be done with it.

But apparently not this Jesus! He is going to go through with it, flogging and all! Oh, I pity his back when the soldiers finish with that whip I made. *(He works the hide a minute more. He becomes thoughtful.)* He's either a fool ... or I am. *(The actor hangs his head, puts down the tools, and walks out of the room in silence.)*

The Testimony Of The Basket Maker

(The actor or actress is working on twisting a crown of thorns hidden from the audience as the drama begins. He or she sits with back facing the audience. There are baskets and basket-making materials scattered around for effect. There may even be a basket half made or half taken apart to give the suggestion that it is in the process of being made. The actor/actress is seen on stage as an older person, bent and withered from years of sitting in the hot sun. The crown remains hidden from view throughout the opening lines.)

 (Still with back turned but talking to the audience) I have just about finished what I'm doing here. A few more twists should do it. I know that nobody will believe me if I just tell you outright about what I did today, especially my wife/husband. Oh, she/he thinks I have come home over the years with far too many tall tales for her/him ever to believe a thing I say anymore. Most of the time she's/he's ... OUCH, that's sharp ... most of the time she's/he's right. But, today ... today something very peculiar happened while I was in Jerusalem. I know you won't believe me. That's why I'm working on this. Ah, that should about do it. *(The actor/actress turns to show the congregation the crown of thorns.)*

 I felt like I needed to make another one of these crowns to show to you folks and to my wife/husband. Otherwise, who'd believe that this could be worn by someone? That's right. A crown of thorns just like this one was put on a man's head up there at the governor's place today. I couldn't believe it myself ... except that I was there when it happened. The soldiers just placed this crown of thorns right on his head and pushed it down until it fit real tight. Oh, it was perhaps the most cruel thing to which I have ever been party. Well, the reason I was there wasn't because I wanted to be. You see, I was just sitting out by the city wall as I do every morning, trying to sell some of my baskets. Actually, today was a very slow day. I wasn't having much luck selling a single one. But as I sat there I saw a crowd gathering off in the distance near the governor's place. It seemed to be a very loud group of people. There was a lot of shouting and chanting going on. I couldn't make out what was being said because they were too far away ... and my hearing isn't so good anymore. So I sat there squinting at the crowd, trying to get a clue as to what might be taking place, when I saw two Roman soldiers coming toward me. They were running and I thought something was happening just past me. But they didn't turn in any direction ... they kept coming toward me. With haste, I started to gather up my baskets because I didn't want any trouble, but before I could get my things together they arrived. One of the soldiers grabbed me by the arm and said, "Come, old man/woman. You are needed." "But my baskets," I protested. "Who will watch my baskets?" "Leave them," the other soldier told me. "You have more important things to make today," he said as they both looked at each other and laughed.

Well, it seemed like it took forever to get up to the governor's place. These old legs don't move as quickly as they used to and I was stiffening with fright. The crowd of people there was even bigger than I thought. The soldiers pushed their way through to the center of the mob, dragging me with them. I then noticed a peculiar man standing with hands bound awkwardly in front of him like this (demonstrates hands crossed at the wrist in front of body) and his clothes all torn and bloodied. The soldiers stood in a circle around him, tossing him from one side of the circle to the other as if they were tossing a coconut — like the children do when they play. Then one of the soldiers who dragged me there put a basket full of branches in front of me. The branches all had long, sharp-looking thorns on them. "Okay, basket maker," barked the soldier, "twist up a crown for the king!" I was confused by the request. "A crown made of branches with thorns?" I thought. "What sort of king would wear such a crown?" Then I heard the things the soldiers were saying as they toyed with the man, tossing him back and forth like a plaything. "Now then, if you are indeed the Son of God, tell us who it was who just hit you? Yeah, King of the Jews, where's your throne? Where's your great army who will protect you?" The soldiers kept laughing and taunting him, saying these

16

insulting things as I stood watching, perplexed about what was happening. "Make the crown," grunted the soldier as he poked my neck with the blade of his sword, "or you die today." So I quickly picked up two branches of thorns and I nervously started to twist them together ... as if I were making a circular basket ... about the size of a man's head. It took me several minutes to complete the crown. It was very painful working with thorns, as I was constantly being pricked and stabbed by them. Finally, I completed the project and the soldier roughly yanked the crown from my hands. I was then pushed back into the crowd and could no longer see the man they taunted.

Soon after losing sight of him, I heard voices making the sound of horns *(makes the sound of a mock horn with hands pressed against pursed lips)* like they were mimicking a royal entry *(make the sound again)* and I listened as the crowd gasped and then cheered. I can only imagine that they must have pushed the crown made of thorns down onto the head of that man in bloody, torn clothes whom they taunted as king. I tried to see him, but I could not. Someone in the dense crowd near me shouted, "Hail! King of the Jews. There is your crown. Wear it and bleed!" I retreated from that place as quickly as these weary old legs would allow.

All day long I have been wondering about what crime it is this poor man could be accused of to deserve such cruel treatment. He seemed harmless enough, yet the soldiers mocked him and the crowd taunted him mercilessly. They called him a king, but it had to be in jest since they treated him ... not like he was a king but more like a rag doll! And the crown they forced me to twist out of thorn branches ... like this one *(holds up crown of thorns for effect)* ... how could anyone torment a man in that way? His crime must be unlike any other to receive such treatment.

So this is what happened to me today. I know my wife/husband and I know she/he wouldn't believe me if I told this story outright. This is why I had to make this second crown to show to her/him. What about you? Do you believe me? Or do you think this is just another tall tale? Oh, but I tell you it's true. This is what they forced me to make, and they put it upon his head and pushed it down to make it fit ... and to make him bleed. I don't know why.

He didn't look to be such a criminal as to deserve this torture. But he must have done something very wrong. Wouldn't you think? That's all I can figure. He must be a horrible, wicked man for them to treat him so. I must admit, when I saw him ever so briefly ... he looked harmless enough. But it just goes to show that one cannot judge a man based solely on his appearance. That man must be wretched to his core.

The Testimony Of The Blacksmith

(The scene begins with the actor standing over his anvil, pounding out a nail with tongs and a hammer. The clang of the hammer against the anvil establishes the scene.)

I have been at my trade for a good many years, but until today I thought I could say I had seen it all. You see, my family has been forging metals for generations now. I have been standing at this anvil every day for nearly 43 years. So, between me and my father, his father, his father's father and so on ... we have worked with just about every kind of metal and we have forged just about anything to be used for just about any kind of purpose I could think of under the sun. Well, that's what I would have said until today. *(Goes back to hammering for moment.)*

Can you see what I'm making here? Those of you who are close may recognize that I am hammering out a nail. It's a simple procedure, really. All you do is heat the soft iron until it glows an orange-red glow. A good forger of metals will know when the metal is just right for shaping because the iron will become like the color of the sun just as it is about to pass under the earth. Then when the iron is heated you shape it with your hammer, using the anvil to straighten it upon. I have made many nails in my 43 years. I have forged nails out of every conceivable metal. Silver and gold. I have forged them out of bronze and brass. Usually, I forge nails out of the black metal — iron — like this one. So, you see, I have made a lifetime of nails, and like I said earlier, there is nothing I thought I hadn't seen ... until today. What would you think if you were requested to make nails for the purpose of pounding them through human flesh? Ah, you see, you would be stunned as well as I ... but that's what happened to me earlier this morning.

I was lighting the forge to begin my day's work. One of the soldiers from the Roman guard came into my workshop with a request that I make something quite unusual for him. At first I thought he must have seen the beautiful bronze breastplate I had just completed for another soldier. But he assured me his request was much more simple. He wanted me to make three nails for him. That's all. How easy, I thought, as I handed him three simple nails which I had already made the day before. He handed them back, saying they were too small. Then he described just exactly what it was he came to get from me. I couldn't believe my ears. The soldier said that later in the morning there was going to be an execution ... another crucifixion. He said that the man whom they were to execute was sent to them under a very unusual circumstance. The soldier said that they were not going to simply hang him as they normally do, with his hands and feet secured to the beams of a cross by rope. *(Pauses and redirects his conversation)* Are you aware of the common practice of crucifying a criminal? Perhaps before I continue I should explain.

The criminal is bound with rope by the wrists and ankles securely to a cross. In order to take a breath, he must push up with his feet and pull with his arms. Eventually, the criminal falls prey to fatigue and once that happens, he no longer has the strength to push with his legs or pull with his arms to take a breath ... so he suffocates. It usually takes several days to die that way. This is the common practice for an execution by crucifixion. But, according to this soldier, they not only wanted to fasten this unusual criminal to the cross with rope, they also wanted to drive nails through both his hands and feet. Yes, that's why I couldn't believe my ears when he told me he wanted me to make nails for this purpose ... I've never received such a request. I asked the soldier what the man's crime was to deserve this bonus torture. Do you know what the soldier said in his response? He said, "I'm not certain." "I'm not certain?" I repeated back to him. *(Quite surprised by the response, he continues.)* "You're going to hammer nails into a man and you don't even know why?" "Well," the soldier thought for a moment, "it has something to do with this man thinking he's God, or something. I guess he's stirring up a lot of problems in Jerusalem among his own people, the Jews," the soldier continued to say. I considered what the soldier said. In light of some of the most recent outbreaks of rioting and the population's general discontent, it wouldn't be beyond the realm of possibility that the Romans would execute a Jewish militant. So I said to the soldier, "Is this Jewish man you are going to execute trying to lead a revolt against Rome?" The soldier said, "I don't think so. Really, I think his crime is that he says he is God, or the Son of God or something." I replied, "You're right. This is an unusual circumstance."

Well, it took me only a short time to forge the nails he wanted. Like I said, it's a fairly simple procedure. And while I was pounding the nails out, the soldier and I talked about our impression of how volatile our society seems to be these days. The Jewish people are a very proud people and they obviously haven't taken too well to the Roman occupation of this area ... especially Jerusalem. There is a lot of tension over this issue. The Jewish people are also an extremely religious-oriented people and it seems that everything the Romans do disturbs their religious way of life. In fact, there have been several uprisings among the people lately led by a militant band of armed gypsies promising to take back what they say is rightfully theirs ... "The land God gave to us," they claim.

I also mentioned to the soldier that I have heard about a man from Galilee — a Jewish person who was gaining quite a substantial following in the area for his religious teachings. The people call him a rabbi, which I believe is a teacher. But what I have been hearing, none of which the soldier knew anything about, is that this rabbi has been leading a sort of peace movement amongst his people, particularly here in Jerusalem. Although this rabbi seems to levy a considerable amount of criticism concerning the Roman occupation, even more strange than that, he highly criticizes the religious leaders of his own people. Now, from what I understand, this rabbi is constantly challenging the religious leaders, saying they are not being faithful to God. He says they are after their own gains and only out for their own self-interests. Well, the reason why I tell you this is that, in the midst of talking with the soldier about all that's happening, and especially this impending crucifixion, it occurred to me that I have heard of this rabbi from Galilee I speak of being referred to as the one sent by God. He's even been called the Son of God. So, I asked the soldier if he thought it might be this particular rabbi who they would be executing. He said he didn't think so, but he added that he really didn't know much about the specifics. Maybe he was ... maybe not. He didn't know. The soldier did say that his impression of the man is that he is not much of a leader. He said that most of the people who were witnessing his execution trial before the governor seemed to be against him and they also seemed satisfied with the proceedings toward crucifixion.

After the soldier left with the nails, I got to thinking about people in general and this rabbi specifically. Now, it may or may not be the rabbi I'm thinking of whom they are executing today. But if it is, I would really have to question why. From what I have heard and I admit I only hear bits and pieces from people who come into my workshop ... but what I hear is this rabbi from Galilee speaks about a Kingdom of God. Now, even though I may look sooty and sweaty from my work, I pride myself on being a philosopher of sorts. I can afford a lot of time applied toward philosophical thinking while I stand here pounding on metal. So what this rabbi has to say about a Kingdom of God ... well, it intrigues me. Now, the rabbi says that this Kingdom is not of this world but it is the Kingdom of Heaven. However, the rabbi also suggests that people can be a part of this kingdom even as they live in this world. How, you might ask? Well, this is where I would question the legitimacy of his execution. This rabbi says that people can be a part of the kingdom of God by loving their enemies; by giving to poor people; by being humble; and by believing in him. Now, does any of that sound like justification for an execution? Not in my mind. It sounds to me like this rabbi is simply promoting an attitude for living a peaceful life. So, you see, it makes me wonder about people. If it is, in fact, this particular rabbi they are executing for claiming to be the Son of God as the soldier said, then what do people want? If they truly want to live in peace, then why don't they listen to this rabbi? Instead, they choose to have him killed? They must be like the soldier who came for those nails ... they don't have a clue about what they are doing or why. Well, if it is this rabbi from Galilee, it would be interesting to know what he thinks about these people who are doing this to him. My guess is he's given up on this peace movement, and now he's cursing the people all the way to the cross and, I'm certain, even to his dying breath. (Goes back to hammering for a moment ... then exits.)

The Testimony Of The Carpenter

(The acting area is set with carpentry tools scattered about. The carpenter is planing one of the beams of the cross. During the presentation, the carpenter and two helpers will put the cross together and tie the cross beams with rope.)

You will excuse me if I appear tired tonight. It has been an exceptionally long day for me. These old bones hurt and I have a bit of a headache. I suppose I must be getting too old to handle the sort of commotion I had in here today. Oh, but you don't want to listen to an old man complain. *(Pauses to plane the wood)* You see, this is my carpentry shop. Here is where I have spent the last 51 years of my life. I can tell you — I have seen days come and I have seen days go, but today is one like I never want to see again ... ever.

But before I get into that, let me show you what I am working on here. I am planing the groove on this beam of wood so that it will fit snugly into the groove of this other beam of wood. Have any of you ever seen a cross? That is what the finished product will be once these two beams of wood are fitted and bound together with rope. Then the soldiers of the Roman army will take this cross and carry it just out of town to a hill they call "The Place of the Skull." Believe me, this is a fitting title for such a place. It gives me goose flesh just to mention it. The Place of the Skull is the location where criminals are taken and executed. They are hung on a cross, like this one, for a torturous death by slow suffocation *(shudders)*. Oh, I would rather not talk about that if you don't mind. It really is very gruesome.

You are probably wondering then why it is that I make these crosses, if what they are used for repulses me so. That's a good question, and I probably don't have a good answer for you. All I can say is I have been a carpenter all my life and I am just too old to fight. I have been chosen, you could say — commissioned by the Roman military — to make these crosses for them. To refuse ... well, as I say ... I am just too old to face the consequences.

I come from a long line of carpenters. My father likes to tease my grandchildren. That would be my children's children. He tells them that our family has been in the carpentry trade since Noah. He tells them that Noah was the greatest carpenter who ever lived. My father loves to tell illustrative tales to the children about how large the ark was that Noah made. In fact, my father made a small model of the ark to use in his re-creation of the story of the great flood. The great-grandchildren marvel at the story just as my children's children did, as my children did, as I did ... and still do. Holding up his model ark filled with all the animals he spent days whittling, my father tells the story with such conviction. *(Dramatically)* "In the six hundredth year of Noah's life, in the second month, on the seventeenth day of the month, on that day all the fountains of the great deep burst forth, and the windows of the heavens were opened. The rain fell on the earth forty days and forty nights." *(Pausing in a state of deep reflection)* Seems just yesterday when we were all so young. My father can no longer work with the wood. He's too old, just as I will be very soon. *(Less lightheartedly)* My father is quite unhappy with these crosses I make. He says they are a waste of God's good creation. *(Dramatically)* "Trees were made to provide shelter for God's creatures and to sustain life," he says, "and now they are cut down and you turn them into instruments of death? Shame on you, my son." Well, some days I can just shrug his words off as the ranting of an old man. But, today ... well, today his words haunt me.

Three soldiers barged into my tent early this morning demanding that I give them three crosses. I had heard that two thieves would be executed this week, so in anticipation of their request, I had already produced two crosses. However, the soldiers laughingly told me that they had sentenced to death another. They obviously were in need of three crosses instead of two. So they left here with the two, saying they would return for the completed third cross in the morning. The one I am working on is that third one. I asked them, as they were leaving, who the other thief was they would crucify. They informed me that he was no thief at all ... he was a king, they said. "King of the Jews," they laughed. Well, this sarcasm caught me off guard since I am a Jew and know of no such king among my people. I followed the soldiers out of the tent, imploring them to tell me the name of this king. "Jesus of Nazareth," they told me as they ran off. As I turned to walk back in to my shop it dawned on me that I have heard of this Jesus of Nazareth. In fact, I have heard him speak in person. Briefly. Just a few days ago in Jerusalem, he was speaking to a crowd. I was passing through on my way to market when I heard this man quoting the words of our prophet, Isaiah. I must admit that I have not been devout in my religious practice for a long time. But I remember the words of our prophets from my learnings as a child. This man was quoting Isaiah and saying strange things I did not understand. He said something like, "Whoever believes in me believes not in me but in the one who sent me. And whoever sees me sees him who sent me." He said something about not coming to judge the world but to save it. I inquired from someone in the crowd who this man was who was speaking. They told me he was a rabbi, Jesus, from Nazareth. That did not strike me as odd since there are many rabbis who roam the land teaching in each city as they go. But then, as I recall, this Jesus of Nazareth said something peculiar. He said he does not say the things he says on his own but the Father who sent him commands him about what to say.

Now, as I mentioned, what I heard from this Jesus was very brief and I did not quite understand it all. But something in his voice was quite powerful. I remember thinking how the power and authority with which he spoke seemed to make the prophet's words he used come alive! And the things he said following them, though I did not understand their meaning, seemed to have the ring of truth in them. I heard people in the crowd say that this Jesus is the one who has been healing the sick and forgiving the sins of people in the region. When I encountered Jesus earlier this week it was the first time I had even heard of him. Now this very morning, just a few days later, these soldiers tell me that this same Jesus who was speaking in the town center would be hung alongside two convicted thieves to suffer perhaps the most cruel death I could ever imagine? I am a bit mystified about it all. Could I have misjudged this wonderful speaker so greatly that he is really no more than a criminal?

I remember the crowd in Jerusalem that day was very large and as I stood listening to him, I was caught up in a surge which carried me to where I no longer was within hearing distance. I fought to get back to where I could hear, but it was no use. The flow of people made it too difficult. I thought to myself that perhaps another opportunity would come for me to hear him. Yet that day I would have liked to linger for a while and listen to what this rabbi from Nazareth was saying. I felt at the time that something in his voice seemed quite authentic ... full of authority. I had a sense that he was speaking words I needed to hear. Listening to him that day reminded me that I have been in search of something throughout my life which I know I have never really been able to find ... something missing. I am probably too old now to ever find it, but I have always prayed for a chance. I feel like I might have had that chance if I could have only heard and perhaps understood more of what this Jesus had to say. I suppose I won't get the chance now. As I mentioned earlier, a cloud of foreboding has been lingering over me all day long. I feel a sense of regret that I will not have the opportunity to hear the words and teachings of the rabbi Jesus. He will be executed ... crucified for a crime that I know nothing about. *(Full of remorse)* And what's more, he will hang on a cross that I made with my own hands.

So, do you understand why my sense of remorse is great? My father's admonition over this cross-making business has caused me to be quite disturbed this day. Particularly since I know it will be upon this one that the rabbi Jesus will hang. Have I made a grave mistake by agreeing to make these crosses ... this cross? His message seemed to be very powerful and, if what they say about his healing and forgiveness is true, am I now to be responsible for its termination? Is my cross to be the end of Jesus? God help me.

The Testimony Of The Stone Mason

(The scene begins with the actor standing with a chisel and a hammer, chiseling a block of stone.)

A very wealthy man from Arimathea came to me several seasons ago. He wanted me to carve a tomb out of the side of a rock hill for him. At first, I had my doubts about such a request. But after he told me how much he was willing to spend for my services ... well, I knew at that point I could work something out. So the wealthy man and I went to see the hillside out of which he envisioned this tomb could be hewn. "It's solid rock," I thought to myself. "This will take an eternity for me to chisel out enough space for someone to be buried in here." However, since the man from Arimathea said he was willing to pay me daily while I worked on his tomb AND upon completion he promised a large bonus ... how could I refuse? *(Continues to chisel on the stone)*

I only completed my work on the tomb earlier this week. It has taken me many seasons since that wealthy man first approached me until I finished his confounded tomb. I tell you I did nothing else the entire time. All my regular business and projects were either scrapped, or put on hold, or people sought out other masons to do work for them. But even though I lost a lot of clients, I broke most of my tools, and my back will never be quite the same from working in such awkward positions ... the man from Arimathea paid me handsomely. I will never want for anything ever again.

So really the wealthy man who paid me to hew the tomb for him did me quite a favor. Now I can pick and choose what jobs I want to do and which ones I want to refuse. In fact, having a nice big financial nest egg has freed me up to be more selective in my artistic work. I no longer have to simply shape stones for walls or for building structures. Now I work only on ornamental columns for the palace of the governor or the other rich Romans in the area. My favorite masonry work is done on these ornate capitals ... which is what I am working on here. This particular piece will be placed

27

on the top of a pillar which is located in the antechamber of the governor's bathing room. I also chisel out the columns and pilasters upon which these ornate capitals sit ... but working in detail on creations such as this is what I truly love. It's artistic. Heaven forbid I should ever be forced to hew out another one of those tombs. There is nothing artistic about that sort of work. Except, of course, for the seal. That I am quite proud of. The seal is the stone which I cut into a rounded shape so that several very powerful men could roll it to close up the tomb. It took a very long time to calculate it just right and to shape the stone so it would fit tightly into the tomb opening. That was as much artistic work as was required of that job. Otherwise, each day I worked on the tomb was routine.

Unlike working in detail on these capitals, which I consider to be creating art, chiseling that tomb was tediously monotonous and boring ... and besides, it was creepy. After all, I sat or laid down in that tomb for many, many days in a row. My friends joked with me telling me that I'm lucky. "Just think of the poor dead loser who will be put in there after he dies," they reminded me. "Unlike that one, at least you get to walk out of the tomb alive every day." I suppose they had a good point. But they might think differently if they knew what I know now. *(Becoming more sober)* I tell you, I just cannot figure it out. I spent months working on that tomb and there is no way that once that sealing stone was placed at the opening any one man could roll it away and open the tomb.

Well, anyway, chiseling out a tomb for all those days with all that time to myself to think, I was prompted to consider the meaning of death and dying. I am a fairly young man in good health, so I have never really given it much thought. But when you're in a tomb for so long ... well, it's hard not to think about death. I am no expert on how the body works, but I have observed that, in order to keep living, my body has to breathe in and out. Even though I can't see what is going in my body or what is coming out, I know that I am bringing something into my body which is necessary to sustain my life. Breathing has something to do with keeping me alive. Also, I have had many cuts in my skin on several parts of my body over the years and I have noticed that each time the skin is cut, blood oozes out. My grandmother used to say, "Blood is God's tears and the tears are medicine, so that when your skin is cut, God is crying to heal your wound." I understand that blood too has to have something to do with keeping me alive. I know this because I have seen when people die. They no longer breathe and their blood stops flowing. Life is a very powerful thing indeed. But my experience tells me that death is even more powerful, because in the end, life always seems to give up to death. So the reason this rich man from Arimathea paid me handsomely to hew a tomb in the side of that rock hill was for the purpose of placing a body in it which had stopped breathing and bleeding ... a body which had no more life in it ... a body which was dead. He said it was meant to be *his* tomb someday.

This morning I received word from a neighbor that this wealthy man from Arimathea placed someone else's body in the tomb. Apparently this someone else was a criminal who had been crucified on Golgotha a few days ago. My neighbor says that this criminal had been given the extreme treatment as far as punishment goes. She says he had been flogged, they had cruelly put a crown made of thorns on his head and dressed him in a scarlet robe mocking him as some sort of king, they had beat him with their fists, and finally, they crucified him by nailing his hands and feet to a cross of wood. She says it took only three hours for him to die. Then, my neighbor tells me that a very wealthy man from Arimathea, along with several women and a few men, had the body taken down off the cross and carried to a tomb ... as you may have figured out, the tomb which I have just finished. They placed the body in it and rolled the rounded stone I worked so hard to shape in front of that tomb to seal off the opening.

My neighbor says that Roman soldiers were placed at the tomb to guard it from anyone getting in and anyone getting out. I had to question her about the anyone getting out part. "Wasn't he dead?" I asked. "Of course he was dead," she assured me. "But before he died there was some talk that he said he would come back to life after three days." "Come on," I said. "Who was this man to say such things?" My neighbor went on to say that this person who had been crucified and was now buried in that tomb was claiming to be the Son of God. And people were rallying around his many signs that he might come back to life. He had been healing the ill and lame. He had been forgiving the sins of the humble in God's name. He had been telling people that the kingdom of God was very near. He said they could witness it in him and in the things that he did and in the words that he spoke. And people were suggesting that this was the one for whom they had waited to free them from their sin. And, according to my neighbor, this Son of God person promised that on the third day of his death ... he would rise back out of his grave. So that's why the Roman guard. But I can tell you, once that stone is set in front of that tomb ... it will take no less than ten men to move it again. He's not coming back out of there. Besides, I said that life is a powerful thing but death is even more powerful. I can't even begin to imagine the sort of power it would take to come back to life from death. Why, that sort of power ... could come from only one source I know of ... that would be from God. And this Son of God person they crucified. Why would the wealthy man from Arimathea bury him in his very own newly-hewn tomb? He was supposed to be a criminal. Wasn't he? Well ... it doesn't matter. That's the rich man's business. Besides, there is absolutely no way the dead man is coming back out of that tomb. So I guess my friends were right. At least I got to walk out of that tomb alive. This Son of God person surely will not. *(Lays down utensils deliberately ... then exits.)*

Five Poems
For
Congregational Recitation

This Little Swatch Of Leather

This little swatch of leather
    I hold here in my hand,
reminds me of the agony
    our Lord did withstand.

It reminds me of the whip
    by which stripes he did bear,
For my brokenness and sin
    though I wasn't even there.

I am reminded that his wounds
    are reaching into my soul,
where they heal me and cleanse me
    so once more I can be whole.

His humble blood, I am reminded,
    at the flogging was spilled
for our lives ... so empty ...
    are needing to be filled ...

... by a love so unswerving
    through pain and in death.
Of the hope in believing
    in Jesus I'll find rest.

Of the joy in knowing
    that a Savior did come,
is coming, will come,
    to restore us as one ...

... with God our creator.

So, this little swatch of leather
    I hold here in my hand,
reminds me that Christ loves,
    like none other can.

Thorns So Sharp And Angry

In my hand I hold a branch,
    its thorns so sharp and angry.
Of such a branch a crown was made
    to add to Jesus' agony.

In a garden he was arrested,
    a cup he didn't choose,
and then they scourged and scoffed at him
    and called him "King of the Jews"!

They placed the crown upon him,
    thrust down onto his head,
then stood to laugh and spit on him
    as blood flowed freely red.

Then dressed him in a garment,
    a scarlet robe for royalty,
they placed a scepter in his hand
    — a reed — then bent their knee.

They taunted him as King,
    treating him like a fake,
but there he stood, the Son of God,
    whose life they soon would take.

Our Lord's humiliation
    began that awful day.
The Lord of love and kindness was
    put on mock display.

Yet he never abandoned love
    for those who pierced his brow
and though our thorns of hate and sin
    pierce him even now.

Our Lord even now continues
    to claim us with his strife
purchased with his pain and death —
    in him we have our life.

And so this branch of thorns,
    as sharp as they may be,
reminds me, the unswerving love
    Christ Jesus has for me.

They Pounded The Nails
With A Hammer

They pounded the nails with a hammer
 sunken deeply in hands and feet.
They pounded the nails with a hammer
 and hanged him up in defeat.

They pounded the nails with a hammer,
 piercing him — making him bleed.
They pounded the nails with a hammer,
 fulfilling this dastardly deed.

They pounded the nails with a hammer,
 a force-driven clang in the air.
They pounded the nails with a hammer
 as a chill caught everyone there.

They pounded the nails with a hammer
 and propped him up high on the hill.
They pounded the nails with a hammer;
 the whole earth seemed to stand still.

They pounded the nails with a hammer,
 then placed on the right and the left.
They pounded the nails with a hammer —
 two criminals guilty of theft.

They pounded the nails with a hammer
 and watched as he struggled to breathe.
They pounded the nails with a hammer
 as the women below him grieved.

They pounded the nails with a hammer
    and hanging there three hours that day.
They pounded the nails with a hammer —
    he eventually died that way.

They pounded the nails with a hammer
    but before his spirit left him —
They pounded the nails with a hammer —
    he called out to God, *"Forgive them ...*

for they do not know what they are doing."

This Cross

This cross I hold reminds me
    on one such Jesus sighed —
for three long hours one Friday
    he gasped for breath, then died.

This cross I hold reminds me
    the sorrow and grief he bore
for all our earthly failures
    which death could claim us for.

This cross I hold reminds me
    God's love's uncompromised
by our grave lack of judgment
    in the ways we live our lives.

This cross I hold reminds me
    that we're freed now from our sin
for by Christ's crucifixion
    our hope's restored in him.

This cross I hold reminds me
    of the hope we now possess
that when this life is over
    we will rest as heaven's guest.

This cross I hold reminds me
    all struggles we now can bear
for with Jesus as our strength
    we know we will get there.

This cross I hold reminds me
    of the way we must concede
as Christ's love grows inside us
    we shall reach toward others' need.

This cross I hold reminds me
    there's a lot of work needs done
in this old world which is hurting
    for the peace and hope of One.

This cross I hold reminds me
    of the promise we will exchange
with people whom we encounter
    for by love our lives are changed.

This cross I hold reminds me
    there is nothing can tear us apart
not disease, nor hate, nor evil
    from the Passion of Christ — God's heart.

For I am convinced that nothing can separate us from the love of God in Christ Jesus our Lord. (Romans 8:38-39)

A Stone So Mighty

A stone so mighty was hewn
    to seal our Lord up in a tomb
taken down off the cross and wrapped in linen
    his body lay in death's womb.

A stone so mighty was placed
    and they made it secure in haste
for the day was near over, the Sabbath begun —
    of time there was little to waste.

A stone so mighty was made
    making certain his body stayed
for before his life ended he told them he'd rise
    to walk back out of his grave.

A stone so mighty was cut
    and rolled to shut life out.
Then soldiers were summoned to guard the tomb
    his power they did not doubt.

A stone so mighty was not
    able to do what they thought.
It couldn't defeat the love of our Lord
    whom Death, in our place, for us fought.

A stone so might was rolled
    a time in history so bold.
They found the tomb empty, the stone rolled away
    the third day — so the story is told.

A stone so mighty was found
  with an angel who wore a white gown
saying, "Women, fear not, for the Lord has been raised.
  Now go tell his brothers in town."

A stone so mighty was given
  to display the power of heaven
that death has no sting, we will live again
  in our Lord Jesus Christ's resurrection.

*For if we have been united with him in a death like his,
we will certainly be united with him in a resurrection
like his.*   (Romans 6:5)

www.ingramcontent.com/pod-product-compliance
Lightning Source LLC
Chambersburg PA
CBHW060809040426
42331CB00046BB/2296